LOW POTASSIUM FOOD GUIDE

A Concise Food List Guide to Keep Your Heart and Kidneys Healthy

Dr. Frazier Gregory

All rights reserved.

No part of this book may be used or reproduced in any form whatsoever without written permission except in the case of brief quotations in critical articles or reviews.

Copyright © 2023 by Dr Frazier Gregory

Disclaimer

The information in this book should not be used to diagnose or treat any medical condition. Not every diet and exercise regimen are suitable for everyone. Before beginning any diet, taking any medication, or beginning any fitness or weight-training program, you should always consult with a competent medical expert. The author and publisher expressly disclaim any and all liability that may arise directly or indirectly from the use of this book. When using kitchen tools, operating ovens and burners, and handling raw food, always use common sense and safety precautions. Readers are encouraged to seek professional assistance when necessary. This guide is provided for informational purposes only, and the author accepts no liability for any liabilities coming from the use of this information.

Printed in the United States of America.

First Edition: May 2023

TABLE OF CONTENT

INTRODUCTION 1

UNDERSTANDING POTASSIUM 3

What Does Potassium Do to You? 6
Why a Low Potassium Diet is Necessary 9
Checking Potassium Level in Foods 12
What Level of Potassium is Good for the Body? 14
How to Use This Book 16

POTASSIUM FOOD LIST 19

7-DAY LOW POTASSIUM MEAL PLAN AND RECIPES 35

FINAL THOUGHTS 59

INTRODUCTION

Welcome to the ultimate low potassium food guide! Whether you're dealing with kidney disease or simply looking to improve your overall health, a low potassium diet can help you feel your best. But with so many foods to choose from, it can be tough to know where to start. But don't worry, we've got you covered!

In this book, you'll find everything you need to know about low potassium foods, from why they're important to how to incorporate them into your meals. We'll cover the basics of potassium, including what it does in the body and how much you should be consuming. We'll also explore why a low potassium diet is necessary for some people, and how to check the potassium levels in your food.

Most importantly, we've created a comprehensive guide to low potassium diet by providing a comprehensive list of foods with their potassium content to help you make food choices that best suit your needs.

So whether you're dealing with kidney disease, managing hypertension, or just trying to make healthier choices, and regardless of whether you're a seasoned pro at low potassium eating or just starting out, this book has something for you.

So sit back, relax, and get ready to embark on a low potassium journey that's both fun and delicious. Let's dive in and discover the wonderful world of low potassium foods together!

PART 1

UNDERSTANDING POTASSIUM

Potassium is a mineral that is essential for our bodies to function properly. It helps regulate fluid balance, muscle contractions, and nerve signals. It is also involved in keeping our hearts beating regularly and maintaining healthy blood pressure.

But, as with many things, too much of a good thing can be bad. If you have certain health conditions, such as kidney disease, your body may not be able to process excess potassium properly. In these cases, it is important to follow a low potassium diet to prevent complications.

Let's start with the basics. Potassium is a mineral that is found naturally in many foods. It is also added to some processed foods, such as canned vegetables and soups, and is often used as a salt substitute.

Adults should consume between 2,500 and 3,000 mg of potassium per day, which can vary depending on age, gender, and health status. However, for people suffering from certain medical conditions, such as kidney disease or heart disease, the recommended intake may be lower to prevent complications.

So, why is potassium so important? Well, it helps to regulate the balance of fluids in the body, which is important for maintaining healthy blood pressure and preventing dehydration. It also plays a key role in nerve and muscle function, helping to transmit signals from the brain to the muscles and vice versa.

In addition, potassium is essential for maintaining a healthy heart. It helps to regulate the heartbeat and can lower the chances of heart disease and stroke. Studies have also shown that a diet high in potassium can help to reduce blood pressure and lower the chances of developing kidney stones.

However, for people suffering from certain medical conditions, such as kidney disease, too much potassium in the diet can be harmful. The kidneys are responsible for filtering excess potassium out of the body, but when they are not functioning properly, potassium levels in the blood can become excessively high, leading to serious health complications.

To prevent this, people with kidney disease are often advised to follow a low potassium diet, which involves avoiding or limiting foods with high potassium content. This can be challenging, as many healthy foods, such as fruits and vegetables, are also high in potassium.

Fortunately, there are many low potassium foods that are still nutritious and delicious. Some examples include apples, berries, cauliflower, broccoli, rice, pasta, chicken, and fish. These foods can be incorporated into a healthy and balanced diet, while still maintaining safe potassium levels.

It's also important to note that the way food is prepared can also affect its potassium content. Boiling or steaming vegetables can reduce their potassium content, while baking or roasting can increase it. So, if you're following a low potassium diet, it's important to be mindful of how you prepare your food.

If you're following a low potassium diet, it's important to be aware of which foods contain high amounts of potassium and which ones are low. This book will provide you with a comprehensive list of low potassium foods to make meal planning easier for you.

Remember, following a low potassium diet doesn't have to be difficult or boring. There are still plenty of delicious and nutritious foods you can enjoy. By understanding which foods are high and low in potassium, and making small alterations to your diet, you can still maintain a healthy and balanced diet while keeping your potassium levels in check.

What Does Potassium Do to You?

Potassium is an important mineral that the body needs to work correctly. It is involved in many different processes, from regulating fluid balance to maintaining a healthy heart and body. But what exactly does potassium do to the body, and why is it important? Here's a closer look at what potassium does to the body:

1. Regulates fluid balance: Potassium helps to maintain a healthy balance of fluids within the cells and tissues, which is essential for proper functioning. When potassium levels are too low, the body can

become dehydrated, which can result in a a range of health problems, including constipation, muscle cramps, and fatigue.

2. Supports nerve and muscle function: Potassium helps to transmit signals between nerve cells and muscles, which is essential for normal muscle contraction and movement. When potassium levels are low, muscles can become weak and may not function properly. This can result in a a range of symptoms, including muscle cramps, weakness, and even paralysis.

3. Maintains a healthy heart: Potassium helps to maintain the electrical activity of the heart, which is essential for proper heartbeat regulation. It helps to regulate the heartbeat and can lower the chances of heart disease and stroke. When potassium levels are too low, the heart may beat irregularly or too slowly, which can be dangerous and even life-threatening.

4. Affects kidney function: The kidneys are responsible for filtering excess potassium from the body, and when potassium levels are too high, this can place a

strain on the kidneys. Over time, this can result in a kidney damage and even kidney failure.

5. Supports bone health: Potassium is also important for bone health. It helps to neutralize acids in the body, which can help to prevent the loss of calcium from the bones. This is important for maintaining strong and healthy bones, especially as we age.

6. Helps with digestion: Potassium is involved in the digestive process. It helps to regulate the movement of food through the digestive system, and can also help to prevent constipation.

In addition to these important functions, potassium has been linked to many other health benefits. Studies have shown that a diet high in potassium can help to lower blood pressure, lower the chances of heart disease, and even lower the chances of stroke. Potassium has also been linked to better muscle recovery after exercise, and a reduced risk of kidney stones.

However, too much potassium in the diet can also be harmful. For people suffering from certain medical conditions, such as kidney disease or heart disease, high potassium levels can be dangerous and can even be life-threatening. That is why it is important to understand how much potassium is right for you, and to work with your healthcare provider to determine a safe and healthy intake. For example, people with kidney disease may need to follow a low potassium diet to prevent complications.

By being mindful of your potassium intake, you can support your overall health and well-being.

Why a Low Potassium Diet is Necessary

Do you know what happens when you have too much potassium in your diet? Well, it's not all sunshine and rainbows, unfortunately. Excess potassium can be harmful to your body, especially if you have certain medical conditions such as kidney or heart disease. That's where a low potassium diet comes in. Here are some reasons why you might need to follow a low potassium diet:

1. Kidney Disease: When your kidneys aren't functioning properly, they can't filter out excess potassium from your body. This can result in a a

dangerous buildup of potassium in your blood, which can cause heart problems and even be fatal. A low potassium diet can help to keep your potassium levels in check and prevent complications.

2. Heart Disease: Potassium is important for a healthy heart, but too much of it in the blood can be a risk factor for heart disease and can also be a problem for people with heart disease. High levels of potassium can cause irregular heartbeats and even lead to cardiac arrest. If you have a history of heart disease, your doctor may recommend a low potassium diet to help reduce your risk.

3. Medications: Some medications, such as certain blood pressure medications, can cause potassium levels to rise. So, if you're taking these medications, your doctor may recommend a low potassium diet to prevent complications.

So, what does a low potassium diet look like? Well, it involves avoiding or limiting foods with high potassium content, like bananas, potatoes, avocados, spinach, and many other fruits and vegetables. Don't worry, though -

there are still plenty of delicious and nutritious foods that you can enjoy!

Some examples of low potassium foods include apples, berries, cauliflower, broccoli, rice, pasta, chicken, and fish. You can still enjoy a variety of foods and flavors, while keeping your potassium levels in check.

It's important to note that everyone's dietary needs are different, and a low potassium diet may not be necessary for everyone. If you're unsure whether a low potassium diet is right for you, talk to your doctor or a registered dietitian. They can help you determine the right dietary plan for your individual needs.

Low potassium diet doesn't have to be boring or tasteless. With a little creativity and some tasty low potassium foods, you can still enjoy a delicious and healthy diet while keeping your potassium levels in check. So, go ahead and explore the wonderful world of low potassium foods!

Checking Potassium Level in Foods

If you're following a low potassium diet, it's important to be aware of the potassium content in the foods you're eating. But don't worry, it's not as complicated as it sounds! Here are some tips on how to check the potassium level in foods:

1. Read the nutrition label: The easiest way to check the potassium level in a food is to read the nutrition label. The amount of potassium in the food will be listed in milligrams (mg) per serving. Be sure to check the serving size, as the potassium content will vary depending on how much you're eating.

2. Use a book or food database: If the food you're eating doesn't have a nutrition label, or you're unsure of the potassium content, you can consult a reliable book or use a food database to look it up. There are many useful books and free online databases that for you to search for the potassium content in foods.

3. Be aware of high potassium foods: Some foods are naturally high in potassium, like bananas, potatoes, avocados, and spinach. If you're following a low

potassium diet, it's important to be aware of these foods and limit your intake.

4. Cook foods in different ways: The way you cook your food can also affect the potassium content. For example, boiling potatoes will cause them to absorb more water and potassium, while baking them will cause some of the potassium to escape. On another hand, soaking potatoes in water before cooking can help reduce the potassium content by up to half. Be aware of how you're preparing your food and how it may affect the potassium content.

5. Consider portion sizes: Even low potassium foods can add up if you're eating large portions. Be aware of portion sizes and try to stick to recommended serving sizes.

Don't be afraid to get creative with your low potassium diet! There are plenty of delicious low potassium recipes out there that can help you stay on track while still enjoying tasty and satisfying meals. Experiment with different spices, herbs, and cooking methods to keep things interesting.

What Level of Potassium is Good for the Body?

So, we've talked about how too much potassium can be harmful, but what about the right amount of potassium? How much potassium is actually good for the body? Well, it all depends on your individual health, and dietary needs.

The recommended amount of potassium to be consumed per day for most adults is around 2,500 to 3,000 milligrams per day. However, this number may be higher or lower depending on factors like age, gender, activity level, and health conditions.

It's important to note that not getting enough potassium can also be harmful to your body. Potassium deficiency, also known as hypokalemia, can cause symptoms like muscle weakness, fatigue, and irregular heartbeat.

On the other hand, too much potassium, or hyperkalemia, can also cause symptoms like muscle weakness, nausea, and even heart failure. That's why it's important to stay within the recommended amount of potassium to be consumed per day.

If you have medical conditions such as kidney disease or heart disease, your doctor may recommend a lower daily potassium consumption to prevent complications. On the other hand, if you're an athlete or someone who sweats a lot, you may need to consume more potassium to help replace the electrolytes lost through sweat.

So, what can you do to ensure that you're getting the right level of potassium for your body? Well, the first step is to talk to your doctor or a registered dietitian. They can help you decide on your personal potassium needs and recommend a dietary plan that works for you.

In general, though, focusing on a balanced and varied diet that includes plenty of fruits, vegetables, and lean proteins can help you get the right level of potassium for your body. And if you need to follow a low potassium diet, there are still plenty of delicious and nutritious options out there.

You can also keep track of your potassium intake using a food diary or app. This can help you stay mindful of how much potassium you're consuming and make adjustments as needed.

While too much or too little potassium can be harmful, staying within the recommended amount of potassium to be consumed per day can help keep your body functioning at its best.

If you're concerned about your potassium intake, it's important to speak with your doctor or a dietitian. They can help you to determine the right amount of potassium for your individual needs, and provide guidance on how to make healthy and balanced food choices.

How to Use This Book

Welcome to your ultimate low potassium food guide! This book is your go-to resource for finding low potassium foods to help you stay healthy and feeling your best with a concisee list of low potassium foods.

But how do you use this book to get the most out of it? Here are a few tips to help you navigate the pages:

1. Start with the basics: Before you dive into the low potassium food list, take some time to read through the first few sections of the book, like "Understanding Potassium" and "Why a Low

Potassium Diet is Necessary." This will give you a solid foundation for understanding why low potassium foods are important and how to make the most of your low potassium diet.

2. Explore the potassium food list: Once you've got the basics down, it's time to dive into the heart of the book - the potassium food list. This comprehensive list includes the potassium value of foods, from fruits and vegetables to meats and grains arranged in alphabetical order for easy access. Use this list to help you plan your meals and make smart choices when grocery shopping.

3. Look through the recipes: Once you've covered the food list, turn to the recipe portion of the book. Our recipes are created to be delicious, filling, and low in potassium, allowing you to enjoy your meals without jeopardizing your kidney health. We have a wide variety of dishes to choose from, including breakfast, lunch, and dinner.

4. Use it as guide to plan your meals: You can use this book to plan your meals and snacks for the day, or to

create a grocery list for your next shopping trip. Simply browse the different food and choose the potassium foods that you enjoy and that fit your dietary needs. Or better still, you can follow the meal plan provided.

5. Keep the book handy: Whether you're at home or on the go, it is always helpful to have this book handy as a reference. Keep it in your kitchen or take it with you when you're out to help you make smart low potassium choices no matter where you are.

This book is your ultimate guide to a low potassium diet, with helpful tips and a comprehensive food list to keep you on track. Use it to educate yourself about potassium content in foods, plan your meals, and make smart choices wherever you go. Whether you're managing a health condition or just looking to make some dietary changes, this book has everything you need to get started.

PART 2
POTASSIUM FOOD LIST

The amount of potassium considered to be high, moderate, or low in a particular quantity of food can vary depending on a number of factors, including the specific food in question and the dietary needs of the individual consuming it.

However, as a general guideline, the following are some rough estimates of what is considered high, moderate, and low amounts of potassium in a 100-gram serving of food:

- High potassium: 500 mg or more
- Moderate potassium: 100-500 mg
- Low potassium: less than 100 mg

Here is a list of common food items arranged in alphabetical order, along with their approximate potassium content per 100 grams or milliliters in the case of liquids.

A:

Abalone (cooked): 486mg

Acorn squash (cooked): 340mg

Adzuki Beans, cooked: 466mg

Agave Syrup: 50mg

Alfalfa Sprouts: 79mg

All-Bran Cereal: 486mg

Almond Butter: 728 mg

Almond Milk (unsweetened): 150 mg

Almonds (raw): 705 mg

Almonds (roasted): 733 mg

Amaranth (blanched): 135 mg

Amaranth (cooked): 332mg

Anchovies (canned in oil): 480mg

Anise Seeds: 1,440mg

Apple Cider: 112 mg

Apples (with skin, raw): 107mg

Applesauce (unsweetened): 102mg

Apricots (dried): 1,101mg

Apricots (raw): 259mg

Arrowroot (cooked): 454 mg

Artichokes (cooked): 370 mg

Arugula: 369mg

Asparagus (boiled): 202mg

Avocado: 485mg

B:

Bagels (plain): 98 mg

Bamboo Shoots (boiled): 533 mg

Bananas (raw): 358 mg

Barley (cooked): 193 mg

Basil (raw): 295 mg

Bay Leaves (dried): 529 mg

Beans, Black (cooked): 305 mg

Beans, Lima (cooked): 358 mg

Beef (cooked, lean): 318 mg

Beet Greens (cooked): 909 mg

Beets (cooked): 325 mg

Bell Peppers (raw): 211 mg

Biscuits: 105 mg

Black Beans (cooked): 422 mg

Blackberries (raw): 162 mg

Blueberries (raw): 77 mg

Bok Choy (cooked): 252 mg

Brazil Nuts (dried/raw): 659 mg

Breadfruit (raw): 490 mg

Broccoli (cooked): 316 mg

Brussels Sprouts (cooked): 389 mg

Buckwheat (cooked): 143 mg

Bulgur (cooked): 123 mg

Butter (unsalted): 24 mg

Buttermilk: 260 mg

Butternut Squash (baked): 352 mg

C:

Cabbage (green, cooked): 170 mg

Cantaloupe (raw): 267 mg

Capers (canned): 2336 mg

Carrots (cooked): 320 mg

Cashew Butter: 553 mg

Cashews (raw): 541 mg

Cashews (roasted): 552 mg

Cauliflower (cooked): 299 mg

Celeriac/Celery Root (cooked): 300 mg

Celery (raw): 260 mg

Cereal (corn flakes): 92 mg

Cereal (oat flakes): 350 mg

Cereal (ready-to-eat): 173-400 mg

Chard (cooked): 549 mg

Cheese (cheddar): 119 mg

Cheese (cottage, 1% fat): 104 mg

Cheese (feta): 143 mg

Cheese(goat, soft): 204 mg

Cheese (mozzarella): 158 mg

Cheese (parmesan): 680 mg

Cheese (ricotta, part skim milk): 167 mg

Cherries (raw): 222 mg

Chestnuts (roasted): 592 mg

Chia seeds: 407 mg

Chicken (breast, cooked): 256 mg

Chickpeas/Garbanzo Beans (cooked): 291 mg

Chili Peppers (raw): 322 mg

Chives (raw): 296 mg

Chocolate (dark, 70-85% cocoa): 715 mg

Chocolate Syrup: 67 mg

Cilantro (raw): 521 mg

Cinnamon (ground): 431 mg

Clams (cooked): 534 mg

Clementines (raw): 177 mg

Cloves (ground): 1027 mg

Cocoa powder (unsweetened): 1524 mg

Coconut (raw): 356 mg

Coconut Water: 250 mg

Cod (cooked): 439 mg

Coffee: 92 mg

Collard Greens (cooked): 223 mg

Corn (cooked): 270 mg

Couscous (cooked): 43 mg

Crab (cooked): 328 mg

Crackers: 45-79 mg (depending on the brand and type)

Cranberries (raw): 85 mg

Cranberry Juice Cocktail: 14 mg

Cream (heavy whipping): 105 mg

Cream cheese: 62 mg

Croissants: 92 mg

Cucumbers (raw): 147 mg

Cumin (ground): 1788 mg

Currants (dried): 864 mg

D:

Dandelion Greens (cooked): 338 mg

Dandelion Greens (raw): 397 mg

Dates (dried): 696 mg

Dates (raw): 656 mg

Dill (fresh): 738 mg

Dill Pickles (canned): 115 mg

Dragonfruit/Pitaya (raw): 436 mg

Duck (roasted): 368 mg

Durian (raw): 436 mg

E:

Edamame (cooked): 482 mg

Eggplant (cooked): 229 mg

Eggs (boiled): 129 mg

Elderberries (raw): 280 mg

Endive (raw): 314 mg

English Muffins: 123 mg

F:

Farro (cooked): 155 mg

Fava Beans (cooked): 362 mg

Fennel (raw): 414 mg

Figs (dried): 680 mg

Figs (raw): 232 mg

Fish (cooked, various types): 250-500 mg

Flaxseed (dried, ground): 813 mg

Flaxseeds: 392 mg

Flour (all-purpose): 115 mg

French Beans (cooked): 209 mg

G:

Garlic (raw): 401 mg

Ginger (raw): 415 mg

Gourd (cooked): 176 mg

Grapefruit (raw): 135 mg

Grapefruit Juice: 139 mg

Grapes (raw): 191 mg

Green Beans/Snap Beans (cooked): 211 mg

Green Peas (cooked): 244 mg

Green Onions/Scallions (raw): 276 mg

Green Tea (brewed): 88 mg

Guava (raw): 417 mg

H:

Halibut (cooked): 490 mg

Hamburger buns: 77 mg

Hazelnuts (butter/raw/roasted): 680 mg

Hemp seeds: 816 mg

Honeydew Melon (raw): 228 mg

Horseradish (raw): 246 mg

Hot Cocoa (made with water): 417 mg

Hot Cocoa (made with milk): 411 mg

Hummus (chickpea dip): 319 mg

I:

Iceberg Lettuce (raw): 141 mg

Indian Gooseberry/Amla (raw): 198 mg

Instant Noodles (cooked): 25 mg

Instant Oatmeal (cooked): 62 mg

Iodized Salt: 11,000 mg

Irish Moss/Sea Moss (dried): 1,022 mg

J:

Jackfruit (raw): 448 mg

Jalapeno Peppers (raw): 320 mg

Jerusalem Artichoke/Sunchoke (raw): 429 mg

K:

Kale (cooked): 296 mg

Kefir: 120 mg

Kiwifruit (raw): 316 mg

L:

Leeks (cooked/raw): 180 mg

Lemonade: 25 mg

Lemons (raw): 138 mg

Lentils (cooked): 369 mg

Lettuce (raw): 141 mg

Lima Beans (cooked): 484 mg

Lime (raw): 102 mg

Lobster (cooked): 367 mg

M:

Macadamia Nuts (butter/raw/roasted): 368 mg

Mackerel (cooked): 444 mg

Mahi-mahi (cooked): 384 mg

Mangoes (raw): 168 mg

Milk (cow's, whole): 150 mg

Milk (cow's, 1% fat): 200 mg

Milk (cow's, skim): 385 mg

Milk (goat's, whole): 204 mg

Milk chocolate: 201 mg

Millet (cooked): 195 mg

Miso (fermented soybean paste): 822 mg

Mushrooms (cooked, various types): 318-420 mg

Mushrooms (Portobello, grilled): 356 mg

Mushrooms (white, cooked/raw): 318 mg

N:

Navy Beans (cooked): 436 mg

Nectarines (raw): 201 mg

Nori Seaweed (dried): 64 mg

O:

Oatmeal (cooked): 125 mg

Okra (cooked): 299 mg

Olives, Black (canned): 88 mg

Olives, Green (canned): 42 mg

Onions (cooked): 146 mg

Orange Juice: 200 mg

Oranges (raw): 181 mg

Oysters (cooked): 215 mg

P:

Pancakes (from mix): 73 mg

Papaya (raw): 182 mg

Parsley (raw): 554 mg

Parsnips (cooked): 375 mg

Passionfruit (raw): 348 mg

Peaches (raw): 190 mg

Peanut Butter: 658 mg

Peanuts (raw/roasted): 705 mg

Pears (raw): 119 mg

Pecans (raw/roasted): 410 mg

Pineapple (raw): 180 mg

Pineapple Juice: 128 mg

Pine Nuts (dried): 597 mg

Pinto Beans (cooked): 373 mg

Pistachios (raw/roasted): 1025 mg

Pita Bread: 110 mg

Pizza Crust: 72 mg

Plantains (cooked): 499 mg

Plums (raw): 157 mg

Pomegranate (raw): 236 mg

Popcorn (air-popped): 329 mg

Poppy Seeds (dried): 719 mg

Potatoes, Russet (baked): 535 mg

Potatoes (cooked): 379 mg

Pretzels: 50 mg

Prickly Pear (raw): 220 mg

Prunes/Dried Plums (dried): 732 mg

Pumpkin (cooked): 340 mg

Pumpkin Seeds (raw/roasted): 809 mg

Q:

Quince (raw): 197 mg

Quinoa (cooked): 172 mg

R:

Radishes (raw): 233 mg

Raisins (dried): 749 mg

Raspberries (raw): 151 mg

Red Cabbage (cooked): 233 mg

Red Kidney Beans (cooked): 406 mg

Rhubarb (cooked): 288 mg

Rice, Brown (cooked): 143 mg

Rice Cakes: 28 mg

Rockfish (cooked): 524 mg

Rye Berries (cooked): 255 mg

S:

Salmon (cooked): 363 mg

Saltine Crackers: 30 mg

Sardines (canned in oil, drained): 397 mg

Scallops (cooked): 375 mg

Sesame Seeds (butter/raw/roasted): 468 mg

Shiitake Mushrooms (dried): 1388 mg

Shrimp (cooked): 195 mg

Sole (cooked): 520 mg

Sour Cream: 105 mg

Soy Milk (unsweetened): 160 mg

Soy Yogurt (unsweetened): 152 mg

Soybeans (cooked): 515 mg

Spelt (cooked): 138 mg

Spinach (cooked): 558 mg

Squid (cooked): 251 mg

Strawberries (raw): 153 mg

Sunflower Seeds (butter/raw/roasted): 645 mg

Sweet Corn (cooked): 270 mg

Sweet Potatoes (cooked): 337 mg

Swiss Chard (cooked): 549 mg

Swiss Cheese (sliced): 140 mg

Swordfish (cooked): 407 mg

T:

Tangerines (raw): 166 mg

Taro (cooked): 591 mg

Tea (black): 88 mg

Tempeh: 212 mg

Tilapia (cooked): 292 mg

Tofu (raw, firm): 147 mg

Tomato Juice: 237 mg

Tomatoes (raw): 237 mg

Tortillas (flour): 88 mg

Tuna (canned in water): 285 mg

Turkey Breast (cooked): 293 mg

Turnips (cooked): 233 mg

U:

Udon Noodles (cooked): 12 mg

Ugli Fruit (raw): 174 mg

V:

Vanilla Extract: 148 mg

Vanilla Ice Cream: 135 mg

Veal (cooked): 325 mg

Vegetable Juice: 220 mg

Venison (cooked): 383 mg

W:

Waffles (from mix): 62 mg

Walnuts (dried/raw): 441 mg

Watermelon (raw): 112 mg

Wheat Bran (raw): 1365 mg

Wheat Germ (raw): 664 mg

Whey Protein Powder: 342 mg

Whipped Cream: 79 mg

White Bread: 55 mg

White Rice (cooked): 35 mg

Whole Wheat Bread: 172 mg

Whole Wheat Pasta (cooked): 24 mg

Whole Grain Tortillas: 117 mg

Wild Rice (cooked): 166 mg

Y:

Yam (cooked): 670 mg

Yellow Squash (cooked): 184 mg

Yogurt(Greek, plain, low-fat): 141 mg

Yogurt (plain, low-fat): 255 mg

Z:

Zucchini (cooked): 261 mg

Note that the potassium content of these foods can vary based on factors such as growing conditions, brand, variety, preparation, and cooking methods, so the values given are approximate and may differ slightly from other sources. Also, some of the foods listed may not be commonly known sources of potassium.

PART 3

7-DAY LOW POTASSIUM MEAL PLAN AND RECIPES

Day 1

Breakfast: Cinnamon Oatmeal (1 serving)

Ingredients:
- 1/2 cup rolled oats
- 1 cup water
- 1/4 cup almond milk
- 1 tablespoon honey
- 1/4 teaspoon cinnamon

Instructions:
1. Combine the rolled oats and water in a medium saucepan over medium flame.
2. Bring to a boil, then reduce the heat and simmer for 5-7 minutes or until the oats are cooked.
3. Stir in the almond milk, honey, and cinnamon.
4. Serve hot.

Nutritional Value: Calories: 206 Carbohydrates: 38g Protein: 5g Fat: 4g Fiber: 5g Potassium: 152mg

Lunch: Chicken Salad (2 servings)

Ingredients:

- 2 cups cooked chicken breast, diced
- 1/2 cup chopped celery
- 1/2 cup chopped onion
- 1/2 cup chopped apple
- 1/4 cup low-fat mayonnaise
- 1 tablespoon apple cider vinegar
- Pepper and salt to taste

Instructions:

1. In a large bowl, combine the chicken, celery, onion, and apple.
2. In a separate bowl, mix together the mayonnaise and apple cider vinegar.
3. Pour the mayonnaise mixture over the chicken mixture and stir to combine.
4. Season with pepper and salt to taste.
5. Serve chilled.

Nutritional Value: Calories: 275 Carbohydrates: 11g Protein: 33g Fat: 11g Fiber: 2g Potassium: 268mg

Dinner: Quinoa and Vegetable Stir-Fry (2 servings)

Ingredients:

- 1/2 cup quinoa, rinsed and drained
- 1 cup low-sodium vegetable broth
- 1 tablespoon olive oil
- 1/2 red onion, thinly sliced
- 1/2 red bell pepper, sliced
- 1/2 yellow bell pepper, sliced
- 1/2 zucchini, sliced
- 1/2 yellow squash, sliced
- 2 garlic cloves, minced
- 1/4 teaspoon ground ginger
- Pepper and salt to taste

Instructions:

1. In a medium saucepan, combine the quinoa and vegetable broth.
2. Bring to a boil over high heat, then reduce the heat to low and simmer for 15-20 minutes, or until the quinoa is cooked and the broth is absorbed.
3. In a large skillet, heat the olive oil over medium-high heat.

4. Add the sliced red onion, red and yellow bell peppers, sliced zucchini, and sliced yellow squash to the skillet.
5. Cook for 5-7 minutes, or until the vegetables are tender.
6. Add the minced garlic and ground ginger to the skillet and cook for an additional minute.
7. Stir in the cooked quinoa and season with pepper and salt to taste.
8. Serve hot.

Nutritional Value: Calories: 252 Carbohydrates: 34g Protein: 8g Fat: 10g Fiber: 6g Potassium: 433mg

Day 2

Breakfast: Egg and Cheese Sandwich (1 serving)

Ingredients:
- 1 whole grain English muffin
- 1 egg, scrambled
- 1 slice low-fat cheddar cheese
- Pepper and salt to taste

Instructions:
1. Toast the English muffin.

2. In a small pan, scramble the egg and season with pepper and salt.
3. Place the cheese slice on the bottom half of the English muffin.
4. Top with the scrambled egg and the other half of the English muffin.
5. Serve hot.

Nutritional Value: Calories: 291 Carbohydrates: 27g Protein: 18g Fat: 12g Fiber: 4g Potassium: 178mg

Lunch: Lentil Soup (2 servings)

Ingredients:
- 1 tablespoon olive oil
- 1/2 cup chopped onion
- 1/2 cup chopped carrot
- 1/2 cup chopped celery
- 2 cloves garlic, minced
- 1 teaspoon ground cumin
- 1/2 teaspoon ground coriander
- 4 cups low-potassium vegetable broth
- 1 cup dried red lentils, rinsed
- 1/4 cup chopped fresh cilantro

- Pepper and salt to taste

Instructions:

1. Heat the olive oil in a large pot over medium flame.
2. Add the onion, carrot, celery, and garlic and sauté until softened.
3. Add the cumin and coriander and stir to combine.
4. Add the vegetable broth and lentils and bring to a boil.
5. Reduce the heat and simmer for 20-25 minutes or until the lentils are tender.
6. Stir in the cilantro and season with pepper and salt to taste.
7. Serve hot.

Nutritional Value: Calories: 248 Carbohydrates: 38g Protein: 16g Fat: 3g Fiber: 15g Potassium: 344mg

Dinner: Beef Stir-Fry (2 servings)

Ingredients:

- 1 tablespoon canola oil
- 8 oz. beef sirloin, sliced
- 1/2 cup sliced bell peppers
- 1/2 cup sliced mushrooms
- 1/4 cup sliced onion
- 1 clove garlic, minced
- 1 tablespoon low-sodium soy sauce
- 1 tablespoon cornstarch
- 1/4 cup low-potassium beef broth
- Pepper and salt to taste

Instructions:

1. Heat the canola oil in a wok or large skillet over high heat.
2. Add the beef and stir-fry for 2-3 minutes or until browned.
3. Add the bell peppers, mushrooms, onion, and garlic and stir-fry for another 2-3 minutes or until the vegetables are tender-crisp.
4. In a small bowl, whisk together the soy sauce, cornstarch, and beef broth.

5. Pour the soy sauce mixture over the beef and vegetables and stir to combine.
6. Cook for another 1-2 minutes or until the sauce has thickened.
7. Season with pepper and salt to taste.
8. Serve hot.

Nutritional Value: Calories: 259 Carbohydrates: 8g Protein: 25g Fat: 14g Fiber: 2g Potassium: 335mg

Day 3

Breakfast: Almond Berry Smoothie Bowl (1 serving)

Ingredients:

- 1/2 cup frozen mixed berries
- 1/2 banana
- 1/2 cup low-potassium almond milk
- 1 tablespoon chia seeds
- 1 tablespoon honey
- 1/4 cup low-potassium granola

Instructions:

1. In a blender, combine the frozen mixed berries, banana, almond milk, chia seeds, and honey.
2. Blend until smooth.

3. Pour the smoothie into a bowl.
4. Top with the granola.
5. Serve immediately.

Nutritional Value: Calories: 349 Carbohydrates: 53g Protein: 7g Fat: 14g Fiber: 11g Potassium: 310mg

Lunch: Quinoa Salad (2 servings)

Ingredients:
- 1 cup cooked quinoa
- 1/2 cup chopped cucumber
- 1/2 cup chopped bell peppers
- 1/2 cup chopped cherry tomatoes
- 1/4 cup chopped red onion
- 1/4 cup chopped fresh parsley
- 1 tablespoon olive oil
- 1 tablespoon lemon juice
- Pepper and salt to taste

Instructions:
1. In a large bowl, combine the cooked quinoa, cucumber, bell peppers, cherry tomatoes, red onion, and parsley.

2. In a small bowl, whisk together the olive oil, lemon juice, pepper, and salt.
3. Pour the dressing over the quinoa mixture and toss to combine.
4. Divide the salad between two plates.
5. Serve chilled.

Nutritional Value: Calories: 194 Carbohydrates: 25g Protein: 5g Fat: 8g Fiber: 4g Potassium: 266mg

Dinner: Baked Salmon (2 servings)

Ingredients:
- 2 salmon fillets (6 oz. each)
- 1/4 cup low-potassium chicken broth
- 1 tablespoon olive oil
- 1 tablespoon chopped fresh dill
- Pepper and salt to taste

Instructions:
1. Preheat oven to 375°F.
2. Place the salmon fillets in a baking dish.
3. In a small bowl, whisk together the chicken broth, olive oil, dill, pepper, and salt.
4. Pour the mixture over the salmon fillets.

5. Bake for 15-20 minutes or until the salmon is well cooked.
6. Serve hot.

Nutritional Value: Calories: 309 Carbohydrates: 1g Protein: 36g Fat: 17g Fiber: 0g Potassium: 533mg

Day 4

Breakfast: French Toast (2 servings)

Ingredients:

- 4 slices low-potassium bread (such as sourdough)
- 1/2 cup unsweetened almond milk
- 2 eggs
- 1 teaspoon vanilla extract
- 1/4 teaspoon ground cinnamon
- 1 tablespoon butter
- Sugar-free syrup (optional)

Instructions:

1. In a shallow bowl, whisk together the almond milk, eggs, vanilla extract, and ground cinnamon.

2. Dip each slice of bread into the egg mixture, coating both sides.
3. In a large skillet, melt the butter over medium flame.
4. Add the coated bread slices to the skillet and cook for 2-3 minutes on each side or until golden brown.
5. Serve with sugar-free syrup, if desired.

Nutritional Value: Calories: 214 Carbohydrates: 19g Protein: 9g Fat: 11g Fiber: 2g Potassium: 129mg

Lunch: Turkey and Cheese Wrap (1 serving)

Ingredients:
- 1 low-potassium tortilla wrap
- 2 ounces low-sodium turkey breast, sliced
- 1 slice low-potassium cheese
- 1/4 cup sliced cucumber
- 1/4 cup shredded lettuce
- 1 tablespoon hummus

Instructions:
1. Lay the tortilla wrap flat on a plate.

2. Layer the sliced turkey breast, low-potassium cheese, sliced cucumber, and shredded lettuce on top of the tortilla wrap.
3. Spread the hummus over the top of the ingredients.
4. Roll the tortilla wrap tightly, tucking in the ends as you go.
5. Cut the wrap in half and serve.

Nutritional Value: Calories: 277 Carbohydrates: 25g Protein: 23g Fat: 10g Fiber: 6g Potassium: 299mg

Dinner: Chicken and Vegetable Skewers (2 servings)

Ingredients:

- 2 boneless, skinless chicken breasts, cut into 1-inch cubes
- 1 zucchini, cut into 1-inch cubes
- 1 yellow squash, cut into 1-inch cubes
- 1 red onion, cut into 1-inch cubes
- 1 red bell pepper, cut into 1-inch cubes
- 1 tablespoon olive oil
- 1 tablespoon balsamic vinegar
- 1 teaspoon Italian seasoning

- Pepper and salt to taste

Instructions:
1. Preheat the grill to medium-high flame.
2. Thread the chicken, zucchini, yellow squash, red onion, and red bell pepper onto skewers.
3. In a small bowl, whisk together the olive oil, balsamic vinegar, Italian seasoning, pepper, and salt.
4. Brush the mixture over the chicken and vegetables.
5. Grill the skewers for 10-12 minutes or until the chicken is well cooked.
6. Serve hot.

Nutritional Value: Calories: 298 Carbohydrates: 12g Protein: 34g Fat: 13g Fiber: 3g Potassium: 631mg

Day 5

Breakfast: Greek Yogurt Parfait (1 serving)

Ingredients:
- 1/2 cup low-potassium Greek yogurt
- 1/4 cup low-potassium granola
- 1/4 cup sliced strawberries

- 1/4 cup blueberries

Instructions:
1. In a small bowl, layer the Greek yogurt, granola, sliced strawberries, and blueberries.
2. Serve chilled.

Nutritional Value: Calories: 233 Carbohydrates: 28g Protein: 16g Fat: 6g Fiber: 3g Potassium: 273mg

Lunch: Egg Salad (2 servings)

Ingredients:
- 4 hard-boiled eggs, chopped
- 1/4 cup chopped celery
- 1/4 cup chopped red onion
- 1/4 cup low-fat mayonnaise
- 1 tablespoon chopped fresh dill
- Pepper and salt to taste

Instructions:
1. In a large bowl, combine the chopped hard-boiled eggs, celery, and red onion.
2. In a small bowl, whisk together the mayonnaise, dill, pepper, and salt.

3. Pour the dressing over the egg mixture and toss to combine.
4. Divide the egg salad between two plates.
5. Serve chilled.

Nutritional Value: Calories: 199 Carbohydrates: 4g Protein: 12g Fat: 15g Fiber: 1g Potassium: 155mg

Dinner: Vegetable Stir-Fry (2 servings)

Ingredients:
- 1/2 cup sliced carrots
- 1/2 cup sliced bell peppers
- 1/2 cup sliced zucchini
- 1/2 cup sliced yellow squash
- 1/2 cup chopped broccoli
- 2 cloves garlic, minced
- 1 tablespoon olive oil
- 1 tablespoon low-sodium soy sauce
- 1 tablespoon honey
- 1/2 teaspoon ground ginger
- 1/2 teaspoon sesame oil
- Pepper and salt to taste

Instructions:
1. Heat the olive oil in a large skillet over medium-high flame.
2. Add the sliced carrots, bell peppers, zucchini, yellow squash, and broccoli to the skillet and sauté for 5-7 minutes or until the vegetables are tender-crisp.
3. Add the minced garlic and sauté for an additional 1-2 minutes.
4. In a small bowl, whisk together the soy sauce, honey, ginger, sesame oil, pepper, and salt.
5. Pour the sauce over the vegetables and toss to combine.
6. Serve hot.

Nutritional Value: Calories: 134 Carbohydrates: 18g Protein: 4g Fat: 7g Fiber: 4g Potassium: 391mg

Day 6

Breakfast: Berry Smoothie (1 serving)

Ingredients:

- 1/2 cup unsweetened almond milk
- 1/2 banana, sliced
- 1/4 cup frozen strawberries
- 1/4 cup frozen blueberries
- 1 tablespoon chia seeds

Instructions:

1. Combine all ingredients in a blender and blend until smooth.
2. Serve chilled.

Nutritional Value: Calories: 175 Carbohydrates: 28g Protein: 4g Fat: 6g Fiber: 9g Potassium: 277mg

Lunch: Tuna Salad Lettuce Wraps (2 servings)

Ingredients:

- 1 can low-sodium tuna, drained
- 1/4 cup chopped celery
- 1/4 cup chopped red onion
- 1/4 cup low-fat mayonnaise
- 1 tablespoon chopped fresh parsley

- Pepper and salt to taste
- 4 large lettuce leaves

Instructions:

1. In a large bowl, combine the drained tuna, celery, and red onion.
2. In a small bowl, whisk together the mayonnaise, parsley, pepper, and salt.
3. Pour the dressing over the tuna mixture and toss to combine.
4. Divide the tuna salad between the four lettuce leaves.
5. Serve chilled.

Nutritional Value: Calories: 119 Carbohydrates: 5g Protein: 14g Fat: 5g Fiber: 1g Potassium: 199mg

Dinner: Baked Salmon with Vegetables (2 servings)

Ingredients:

- 2 salmon fillets (4-6 ounces each)
- 1/2 cup sliced carrots
- 1/2 cup sliced bell peppers
- 1/2 cup sliced zucchini
- 1/2 cup sliced yellow squash

- 1/2 cup chopped broccoli
- 1 tablespoon olive oil
- Pepper and salt to taste

Instructions:

1. Preheat oven to 375°F.
2. Place the salmon fillets in a baking dish.
3. In a large bowl, toss together the sliced carrots, bell peppers, zucchini, yellow squash, broccoli, olive oil, pepper, and salt.
4. Spread the vegetable mixture around the salmon fillets in the baking dish.
5. Bake in the preheated oven for 20-25 minutes or until the salmon is well cooked and the vegetables are tender.
6. Serve hot.

Nutritional Value: Calories: 303 Carbohydrates: 10g Protein: 31g Fat: 16g Fiber: 3g Potassium: 505mg

Day 7

Breakfast: Parfait with Granola and Berries (1 serving)

Ingredients:

- 1/2 cup low-potassium granola
- 1/2 cup plain Greek yogurt
- 1/4 cup blueberries
- 1/4 cup raspberries

Instructions:

1. In a glass, layer the granola, Greek yogurt, blueberries, and raspberries.
2. Repeat the layers until all the ingredients are used.
3. Serve chilled.

Nutritional Value: Calories: 255 Carbohydrates: 38g Protein: 15g Fat: 6g Fiber: 6g Potassium: 235mg

Lunch: Chicken and Vegetable Stir-Fry (2 servings)

Ingredients:

- 8 ounces boneless, skinless chicken breast, sliced
- 1 cup sliced bell peppers
- 1 cup sliced zucchini
- 1 cup sliced yellow squash

- 1 cup chopped broccoli
- 1 tablespoon olive oil
- 2 cloves garlic, minced
- 1 tablespoon low-sodium soy sauce
- 1 tablespoon honey
- 1/2 teaspoon ground ginger
- Pepper and salt to taste

Instructions:

1. Heat the olive oil in a large skillet over medium-high flame.
2. Add the sliced chicken breast to the skillet and sauté for 5-7 minutes or until the chicken is well cooked.
3. Add the sliced bell peppers, zucchini, yellow squash, and broccoli to the skillet and sauté for an additional 5-7 minutes or until the vegetables are tender-crisp.
4. Add the minced garlic and sauté for an additional 1-2 minutes.
5. In a small bowl, whisk together the soy sauce, honey, ginger, pepper, and salt.

6. Pour the sauce over the chicken and vegetables and toss to combine.
7. Serve hot.

Nutritional Value: Calories: 247 Carbohydrates: 23g Protein: 26g Fat: 7g Fiber: 5g Potassium: 482mg

Dinner: Salmon and Asparagus (2 servings)

Ingredients:
- 2 4-ounce salmon fillets
- 1 pound asparagus, trimmed
- 1 tablespoon olive oil
- 1/4 teaspoon garlic powder
- Pepper and salt to taste
- Lemon wedges for serving

Instructions:
1. Preheat oven to 400°F.
2. Line a baking sheet with parchment paper.
3. Place the salmon fillets and asparagus on the prepared baking sheet.
4. Drizzle the olive oil over the salmon and asparagus, then sprinkle with garlic powder, pepper, and salt.

5. Bake in the preheated oven for 12-15 minutes, or until the salmon is cooked through and the asparagus is tender.
6. Serve with lemon wedges on the side.

Nutritional Value: Calories: 278 Carbohydrates: 7g Protein: 29g Fat: 15g Fiber: 3g Potassium: 528mg

FINAL THOUGHTS

Congratulations, you made it to the end of my low potassium food guide! I hope that this book has been a helpful resource for you on your journey to eating a low potassium diet. As a final note, I wanted to leave you with a few thoughts to keep in mind:

1. Eating a low potassium diet doesn't have to be boring! There are plenty of delicious low potassium foods and recipes out there that can help you stay on track while still enjoying your meals.

2. Don't be afraid to get creative in the kitchen. Experiment with different low potassium foods and recipes, and don't be afraid to try something new.

3. Remember that everyone's dietary needs are different, so what works for one person may not work for another. If you have any questions or concerns about your low potassium diet, don't hesitate to reach out to a healthcare professional for personalized advice.

4. Finally, don't forget that a low potassium diet is just one piece of the puzzle when it comes to living a

healthy lifestyle. Be sure to also prioritize regular exercise, stress management, and getting enough sleep to help support your overall health and wellbeing.

I hope that you've found this book to be a helpful resource, and I wish you all the best on your low potassium journey. Thanks for reading!

Printed in Great Britain
by Amazon